The Lemon Tree

Also by Ilil Arbel

Maimonides: A Spiritual Biography

Witchcraft: A History of Wicca

The Cinnabar Box

Ida Rosenfeld, née Wissotzky

The Lemon Tree

Ida Rosenfeld and Ilil Arbel

iUniverse, Inc.
New York Lincoln Shanghai

The Lemon Tree

Copyright © 2005 by Ilil Arbel

All rights reserved. No part of this book may be used or reproduced by any means, graphic, electronic, or mechanical, including photocopying, recording, taping or by any information storage retrieval system without the written permission of the publisher except in the case of brief quotations embodied in critical articles and reviews.

iUniverse books may be ordered through booksellers or by contacting:

iUniverse
2021 Pine Lake Road, Suite 100
Lincoln, NE 68512
www.iuniverse.com
1-800-Authors (1-800-288-4677)

ISBN: 0-595-33982-4

Printed in the United States of America

*To the Wissotzky family and their magnificent dreams,
so many of which were actualized.*

CONTENTS

LIST OF ILLUSTRATIONS xi
INTRODUCTION xv
CHAPTER ONE: SIBERIA 1
CHAPTER TWO: THE SEED 15
CHAPTER THREE: MOURNING 18
CHAPTER FOUR: PREPARATIONS 26
CHAPTER FIVE: THE TRAIN 30
CHAPTER SIX: ESCAPE 34
CHAPTER SEVEN: CITY OF LANTERNS 38
CHAPTER EIGHT: THE SHIP 45
CHAPTER NINE: ANOTHER VARIETY OF SHIP 49
CHAPTER TEN: HOME 57
CHAPTER ELEVEN: SASHA'S DREAM 66
EPILOGUE 69

LIST OF ILLUSTRATIONS

FRONT PIECE: Front Piece: Ida Rosenfeld, née Wissotzky iii

CHAPTER ONE: SIBERIA

1: Hadassa (left) as a university student 8

2: Hadassa as a young woman 9

3: An invitation for the wedding of Hadassa Winitzkaya and
   Avraham Wissotzky 10

4: Biysk, the Siberian town where the Wissotzky family lived 10

5: Hadassa, Avraham and Sasha (sitting on the fence) with young
   relatives 11

6: Ida as a baby 12

7: Sasha, Ida, and Feera 13

8: The children with friends 14

CHAPTER THREE: MOURNING

1: After the illness. Ida's hair had to be cut because of her
   extremely high fever. 22

2: Grandpa Leib (center) with family 23

3: Aunt Rose on a ship, on one of her many trips to Israel 23

4: The girls with an uncle and his baby 24

5: The girls with their uncle and a family friend 25

CHAPTER SEVEN: CITY OF LANTERNS

1: Official papers from the Chinese consulate in Irkutsk 43

2: The Hongkew market in Shanghai 44

CHAPTER NINE: ANOTHER VARIETY OF SHIP

1: On the ship Sikaka-Mara, going to Port Said 55

2: With a group of refugees in Port Said 55

3: A camel caravan in Port Said 56

CHAPTER TEN: HOME

1: A typical apartment house in Tel-Aviv 62

2: Avraham's dental office in Tel-Aviv 62

3: In the park at Yehuda-ha-Levi Street. 63

4: An early lending library card 63

5: Ida with a friend, dressing up 64

6: Sailing on the Yarkon River with friends 64

7: Ida and Ada as teenagers 65

EPILOGUE

1: Dr. Avraham Wissotzky 78

2: A portrait of Feera 79

3: Feera as a young woman 79

4: Ida on the ship heading for France 80

5: Ida in Nancy 80

6: Leibek in Nancy 81

7: Ida's bust, created by an Israeli artist 81

8: Another bust modeled after Ida 82

9: Ida, painted by an Israeli artist 82

10: Allenby Street, 1933 83

11: Leibek's office in Tel-Aviv 83

12: Feera and Moshe Mishory 84

13: At a seaside café in Tel-Aviv 84

14: Ida and Leibek with their children 84
15: Yafa, Ida's childhood friend, a stylish young woman of the 1930s 85
16: Ora, Ida's childhood friend, with Ida's son (right) and her own son 85
17: The Habima Theater in Tel-Aviv 86
18: Ida's and Feera's older children 86
19: Ida's and Feera's younger children 87
20: The sisters 87

INTRODUCTION

A unique, valuable tale is the birthright of every human being. Often it is overlooked, since we are accustomed to the biographies of great people, and read the history of nations. But the personal stories of ordinary people may be, in the end, a better record of life as it was lived in a specific period of time. The preservation of oral histories is important to families, of course, but I believe it goes further and may interest a much larger audience. Some years ago I wrote a biography of a very great man, the philosopher Maimonides. During my research I came to the conclusion that what made this man so interesting to read about was not his relationship with the high and mighty Saladin, or even his magnificent books that have continued to influence Western culture for over eight hundred years. What really touched me were the details that showed his humanity; his undying love for his lost younger brother, a letter to a friend that described Maimonides' exhausting schedule and debilitating fatigue, and his staunch legal defense of a young woman deserted by her callous and unfeeling husband. Such matters do not belong to the celebrated. They might have happened to anyone. In addition, I simply could not tear myself away from the letters of ordinary people found in the *Cairo Geniza* (an extensive collection of documents discovered in a synagogue in Cairo) that revealed so much about daily life in Maimonides' times.

I hope this book supports such a claim. *The Lemon Tree* is the true story of the pioneering Wissotzky (pronounced *Vissotzky*) family, and the extraordinary year they spent on the road on their way from Siberia to Tel-Aviv. It is narrated by Ida (pronounced *Eeda*), the younger daughter. The book is based on her written memoirs, with a lot of additional material taken from her stories, told to me orally over decades. She was a marvelous storyteller. I struggled to keep her distinctive voice, entirely submitting my writing style to hers—and I am convinced that I accomplished my aim.

The Lemon Tree is the first of three books. Eventually, I hope to publish them together as *The Aliya Trilogy*. The other two—*Tel-Aviv* and *Green Flame,* are novels written by the father, Dr. Avraham Wissotzky. They are fiction, but both describe true pioneering experiences. These three books belong together.

As is my custom, prior to submitting the book to the publisher, I ran it by four readers and a professional editor. I chose my victims carefully for this book. Two of my readers have family connections to the Wissotzky family, and knew them well. In addition, they are extremely knowledgeable university professors, and one of them is a historian who lives and works in Tel-Aviv. The third reader is a director of recreation in an establishment that cares for senior citizens. She is constantly involved with oral histories and memoirs, and has developed a serious degree of expertise in this genre. The fourth reader is an artist; she has deep knowledge and interest in history, and is familiar with the period. I asked for feedback and comments, which they generously gave.

As for the editor, I gave him a horrible task. "Fix my mistakes," I commanded, "but do not dare change the narrator's voice!" I can only justify my imperious behavior by the fact that I had to do exactly the same, and between us, Ida's voice is retained, loud and clear.

Many thanks to my editor, Mr. Gregory B. Ealick, and to my readers, Professor Avigdor M. Ronn, Professor Alexander Mishory, Ms. Dianne Ettl, and Ms. Patricia J. Wynne. Their help was invaluable.

—Ilil Arbel

CHAPTER ONE: SIBERIA

We crushed together into the warm entrance hall, pushing each other, laughing and stomping the snow from our boots. Outside, our coachman led the horses into the stables. "Hurry up with your coat, Ida," said Marusia, our nanny. "Your nose is frozen again. We must take care of it immediately."

"My nose always freezes worse than Sasha's and Feera's noses," I wailed. "It's unfair!"

"Redheads with delicate skin freeze worse than other people," explained Marusia patiently for the thousandth time. Papa poked his head out of his dental office, smiling. "Come, I'll rub your nose with snow and put some goose fat on it," he said, coming to hug us. His patient, an old peasant I knew well, followed him. The peasant smiled at me and said kindly, "Never mind your nose, little Ida. Some day you will be the loveliest girl in all Siberia. Here, I have a little present for you, to make you look just like a real princess." He handed me a small lump of raw gold. "I am not so little," I said proudly. "I am almost seven years old. Thank you, Ivan Petrovich. What a beautiful necklace this will make—I will wear it when I grow up and go to balls and parties!" Ivan Petrovich laughed and patted my head.

Gold was present in Siberia in large quantities. Peasants found it in their lands and fields and often, instead of paying with money, they removed a small bag that hung around their necks, took out raw lumps of gold, put them on the table and said: "Doctor, take as much as is due to you." Among the patients visiting Papa's office many peasants paid that way and Papa kept a small collection. But this piece was special. It had a hole naturally formed through it, and seemed shinier than the

1

usual lumps that looked much like golden earth, crinkled and full of little holes. Marusia fished a piece of string from the bottomless pocket of her embroidered apron, strung the gold and hung it around my neck. "And one for Feera, and one for Sasha," said Ivan Petrovich, generously handing out the pieces. He sighed heavily. "Teeth, teeth," he said to Mama who had just stepped in from the dining room, always sympathetic to people's woes. "Believe me, in the days of my father no one had problems with teeth…" He wrapped himself with his heavy fur hat and coat, and lumbered like a polar bear on his long walk home. I always marveled how the peasants managed to walk so comfortably, even on ice, with their feet wrapped in nothing but layers upon layers of rags. The cold never seemed to bother them, though I remember days when the temperature reached fifty degrees below zero!

Papa and I followed him outside to take care of my frozen nose. Papa rubbed it with snow, really hard, then smeared it with fat. The nose started thawing, turned red, and hurt as if pricked with needles. But I didn't care. I felt like a princess with the gold hung around my neck.

*   *   *

My memories from Siberia are of one big party. Taking trips to the woods to collect bluebells in spring and wild berries in summer. In winter, skating on the ice, throwing snowballs, and building huge snowmen with coal eyes. Traveling in troikas, large sleds hitched to three horses. Pushing our little child-size sleds, running madly, then jumping to lie on them and glide for unbelievable distances on the uninterrupted sheets of ice, feeling as if we were flying.

During winter, life naturally concentrated mainly inside the house. The windows in our house were doubled, with two sheets of glass to protect us from the heavy winds. All the cracks in the window frames were covered with thick felt, to retain the warmth inside the house.

Under the dining room window stood a tropical jungle. Mama could raise any plant, anywhere, even in the arctic weather of Siberia. Her strong interest in the life sciences made her study medicine and become a midwife—one of the first generation of women to be admitted into the University in Odessa, where she met and married Papa. Her father was the estate manager of a wealthy landowner and she grew up surrounded by huge orchards, gardens, and private woods. Mama had a special piece of furniture built for the houseplants, shaped like wooden stairs, stained dark brown, and hand rubbed with oil to a high gloss. Diverse plants stood on the stairs, arranged according to height. The rich, dark green leaves moved slightly in the air currents created by the ever-present heat from the giant stove and the occasional drafts when the door was opened. The intricate greenery looked magical against the white world outside.

*   *   *

The next day I woke up early, remembering that this was Sasha's tenth birthday. I knew a big secret—the nature of the best present—and was terribly excited. It was still dark and bitterly cold, despite the stove in every room, and I hurriedly put on my wooly blue dressing gown and furry slippers before running downstairs to the warm kitchen. It smelled of cinnamon and cloves, since Mama was already creating the birthday cake, her arms deep into flour and sugar. No one could make and decorate cakes like her. Later in Israel, during a desperate shortage of eggs, butter, and sugar, she made cakes from powdered eggs, coarse flour and imitation margarine, and they were still the best cakes I ever ate. I remember her melting raw brown sugar with a tiny birthday candle to create decorations on those cakes, and I still firmly believe that if necessary, she could conjure perfectly good food from virtually thin air. She covered Sasha's birthday cake with white frosting and nautical designs in red, blue, and gold; the cook and the maid busily prepared various other goodies.

"Butter!" I said happily. Milk, cheese, and butter were just delivered from the farm that regularly supplied us, still quite frozen from the trip outside, and the cook prepared to put them in the pantry when I grabbed a butter cake and ate it just as it was, raw, sweet, and creamy. I loved nothing better than those round, fresh cakes of butter, wrapped in cabbage leaves. Mama laughed at my strange taste, but allowed me to indulge it. "Did they bring Sasha's present yet?" I whispered conspiratorially, licking my fingers. "Not yet. Marusia will bring it in the afternoon, during the party."

Feera and I put on our best dresses and tied ribbons in our braids. Feera's rich, wavy, dark chestnut hair had never been cut, and at age eight already reached her knees even when braided. She had delicate features, blue-green eyes and golden skin, and I alternately envied and admired her beauty. I despised my own curly red hair and thought I was ugly. To give Feera credit, she tried, again and again, to tell me that everyone thought I was cute, but I didn't believe her—after all, she was my sister, and therefore partial! Sasha put on a sailor suit and hat; I thought he looked quite elegant and mature.

Many children came, accompanied by their parents who were to have their own party in the formal living room. All the children went for a ride in a procession of beautifully decorated troikas, the coachmen singing with us, the nannies playing their balalaikas, and the bells ringing in the quiet woods. The noisy caravan returned in the early afternoon as darkness fell, the stars came out in the velvety black, clear sky, and the cold became unbearable. We ate a sumptuous dinner, and the gorgeous three-tiered cake was served with *kiessel*, a thick, sweet drink made from wild berries that grew in the nearby wood. You dropped a little milk into the kiessel, and the milk traced delicate, branch-like forms all through the dark crimson, thick liquid. Later in Israel, where wild berries did not grow, Mama invented a new kiessel. Incredibly, she reproduced the drink from the red variety of the desert cactus fruit!

Finally it was time for the presents. Mama and Papa came in, followed by a procession of smiling parents and carrying a small, covered basket. With great ceremony, they put it on the table in front of Sasha. He opened it and stood still. A tiny, round, black ball of fur with white markings looked back at him cautiously with its large black eyes. Sasha picked up the little dog wordlessly and tenderly hugged it. The dog snuggled up to him and put its tiny nose in his hand. This was love at first sight, a love that never died. "Is this a boy or a girl dog?" Sasha whispered. "It's a girl," said Mama. "I'll call you Palma," said Sasha to the dog.

Palma was the Russian name for a palm tree. Sasha had great interest in warm countries, particularly in the tales Papa told about Israel, described as the Land of the Palm Tree.

*   *   *

Darkness descended in the early hours of the afternoon and we filled the long evenings with various games, toys, and occupations. Palma became the main interest as soon as she arrived. Sasha acted as the chief caretaker and assigned Feera and me as his helpers. Soon, Palma became the center of a scientific experiment! Sasha wanted to keep her small; he researched and found that she had to be given a daily dose of a minute quantity of ground copper mixed with water. He regularly administered the medicine and Feera and I worked as copper grinders. Hours upon hours we sat by the stove in the dining room, singing about sailors and seafarers as we rubbed copper coins with sandpaper, special stones, and other diverse equipment to produce the powdered copper.

Palma really never grew and remained small, rounded, and black with white markings. Why didn't she grow? Certainly not because of the ground copper; she probably was simply a naturally small breed. Perhaps she had no sufficient time to grow.

Despite the many toys we possessed, most of the games we played were imaginary. Wearing improvised pith helmets, we explored the dining room jungle, Palma prowling about the undergrowth as our trusty black panther. At other times, we sailed majestic galleons to faraway lands. Arranging chairs in a long row to simulate the ship, we would travel the seas, singing sailors' songs and eating, for a reason I cannot remember, quantities of chicken drumsticks. Perhaps Sasha tried to imitate the dry meat sailors had to eat on ships. We waived the drumsticks in the air, sang, and ate for hours.

Best of all, Papa could tell wondrous stories. We didn't know then, of course, that he would eventually write books for children and adults and be published in three languages. Still, we knew a good tale when we heard it. Every evening, without fail, we demanded story time.

"So which story do you want today, children?"

"Aesop's Fables," said Sasha.

"No, Ali Baba," said Feera.

"Both," said I, the peacemaker.

Papa laughed. "Fine. We'll start with the stork that took the bone out of the wolf's mouth." Aesop's fables required special arrangements. We cleared the table and brought paper and Papa's fountain pen. Feera sat on one of his knees, I sat on the other, and Sasha leaned on the table at a contorted angle. Palma sat on one of the padded chairs and went to sleep. "So, as you know, the stork met this horrible fierce wolf in the forest…" and as he spoke, his arms around us, he drew charming illustrations of the events. The stork had extremely long, skinny legs and a funny face with a long beak. She looked very much like one of Mama's friends, a tall, thin lady who happened to have a long, red nose—of course only by accident!

"And now Ali Baba," said Feera.

There were no pictures drawn for Ali Baba, but the story came alive in another way. Papa put everything in context of our own lives. For example, the nearest grocery store was owned by a Tartar gentleman, who habitually wore special, interesting ethnic clothes, and had large earthenware jars for oil, olives, pickles, and herring. So Papa insisted that all the shopping in the Ali Baba story was done at the Tartar's shop, and the thieves used the Tartar's jars to hide in!

"Incidentally," said Papa seriously, "I just did some research, and found out that the translator of the story made a really stupid mistake!"

"What's that?" asked Sasha breathlessly.

"Well, you know Ali Baba's daughter-in-law Morgiana, who saved the whole family?"

"Of course we know Morgiana," I said.

"Well, her name was really Marusia!"

We knew that he was joking, but the story came alive. When he told us about his life, family and adventures in the small town he grew up in, stories from *One Thousand and One Nights*, or any other fairy tale, somehow they always ended in a journey, pioneering to a golden country, with oranges, eternal sun, and beautiful sandy beaches. Papa's azure eyes became very dreamy, and I saw in them pictures of blue sky, orange groves and endless longing.

Papa went to Siberia because he belonged to the rebelling party in Russia in this period. He first tried the location by himself, and to his surprise, found a city, a lively lifestyle, and even culture. He quickly wrote Mama, who was waiting with Sasha in the Ukraine, and soon they joined him; Feera and I were born there. Papa spent eleven years in Siberia, dreaming about a trip to Israel, and the family shared the dream.

Hadassa (left) as a university student

Hadassa as a young woman

10 The Lemon Tree

An invitation for the wedding of
Hadassa Winitzkaya and Avraham Wissotzky

Biysk, the Siberian town where the Wissotzky family lived

Hadassa, Avraham and Sasha (sitting on the fence)
with young relatives

Ida as a baby

Ida Rosenfeld and Ilil Arbel

Sasha, Ida, and Feera

14 The Lemon Tree

The children with friends

CHAPTER TWO: THE SEED

Drinking tea was a ritual. A fat-bellied samovar stood in the center of the dining room table. I believed that it actually lived its private life and ruled over the furniture in the dining room. You always heard the humming of the boiling water, so the dining room felt alive even when no one occupied it. You wanted to get warm? The samovar stood ready and available for your service, and hot rolls came from the kitchen accompanied by creamy butter and jams made of various berries. We didn't use cups or mugs. The fragrant, amber-colored tea was poured into tall glasses, each fitted into a silver filigree holder with a handle. You had to put a spoon into the glass to prevent it from cracking by the boiling-hot drink. Regular sugar was available, but you could also use the traditional sugar cones that hung on racks on the ceiling of every Siberian kitchen, together with sausages and dried herbs. You broke a small piece of sugar from the cone, put it between your teeth, and sucked your tea rather loudly through it. Mama considered it crude and vulgar, but we, the children, loved the giant sugar cones; Papa sometimes sneakily ate it while Mama pretended not to notice.

Sasha always drank his tea with lemon. One day, he suddenly declared ceremoniously: "I will sow this lemon seed!" He fished the seed from his hot tea, sowed it in a small pot, watered it and said: "Here will grow a lemon tree." His voice rang like the voice of a wizard and his hands made special hocus-pocus movements.

I stood awed. I had never seen a lemon tree growing in Siberia; lemons were imported. Anyway, how will such a small seed grow after being submerged in the hot tea? "The heat may actually help the seed to germinate," said Mama, enchanted with the horticultural experiment.

A new interest entered our daily lives: the lemon tree. Sasha put the pot near the large stove in the dining room to keep it warm. He lit a small electric lamp directly over the pot, to simulate the sunlight it needed.

We examined the pot morning, noon, and evening; the waiting seemed very long. Finally I gave up and stopped believing in Sasha's magic. But Sasha went on watering. One morning, when everyone gathered in the dining room for breakfast, I heard Sasha shout: "It's sprouting, the lemon tree is breaking the ground!" I ran to the pot, and indeed, tiny clumps of earth were spread in a circle around a minuscule green dot!

Sasha looked at us proudly. His worries, which grew bigger with every day that passed without a sprouting lemon tree, completely vanished. His self-confidence returned and he reassumed the position of the grand wizard.

"Some day," he said imperiously, "we'll eat the lemons from this tree!"

"Well," said Mama, hesitating, "there may be a little problem here. Citrus trees don't bloom or bear fruit indoors. We don't have a conservatory, and if we plant it outside, the Siberian weather will certainly kill it."

"Ah," said Papa mysteriously. "But who said that the tree will always live in Siberia?"

Sasha looked at him with complete acceptance of the perfect solution, as shared by two dreamers who positively refused to ever let reality stand in their way.

"You plan to do that?" he asked joyfully.

"Why not?" Said Papa, looking at Mama for support in such a botanical matter. "Right, Hadassa? Can a lemon tree travel?"

"It's possible," said Mama, rising to the occasion. "When we go, we will certainly try. Citrus plants are tough, and I can sew special, padded coverings for it."

When Mama said she could do something, then that was that. You knew everything would be all right.

The little lemon tree continued as our center of interest, as if we transferred a whole orchard from Papa's tales into the tiny pot in Siberia. Mama and Papa shared our excitement, and the maids and other servants that worked in our house came to admire the little miracle.

And so the lemon tree grew—and we grew with it. But a few months later a horrible illness struck; all three children contracted scarlatina. In those days, there were no proper medicines for many childhood diseases, and the cruel Siberian weather did not help. You could only nurse the patients, risk your own life, and pray, and that's exactly what our parents and Marusia did. I don't remember much of those desperate days, as I spent most of the time unconscious. The sickness was hard and long and Sasha did not rise from it.

CHAPTER THREE: MOURNING

The lemon tree was orphaned.

Palma was orphaned.

She never accepted Sasha's death. Feera and I were too ill to attend the funeral, but Mama told me later that Palma followed them to the cemetery and started digging his grave to get him out. They took her home, but she returned to the cemetery every day, and continued digging with her tiny paws. She could not withstand the separation, beautiful Palma, and died after a short time, still small. But the lemon tree went on growing. The entire family continued to take care of it with devotion and reverence.

* * *

In the meantime, politics changed, and Papa became involved with Zionism. Constant danger threatened us because the police searched for him, so Papa started devising ways to escape from Russia. His sister and brothers, who had already left Russia and lived in America, wanted him to join them. However, he was determined to follow his dream, a dream shared by the whole family: pioneering to Israel. Incidentally, at that time, long before the independent State of Israel was declared, people called it Palestine. However, as we are all accustomed to the new name, I will keep to it when telling our story.

I do remember two moments when our commitment to pioneering wavered. One was caused by a letter, and experienced by Mama. The other was experienced by Papa, and strangely enough, was averted by another letter.

Feera and I sat at the dining table, drawing pictures. Papa read the newspaper. Mama walked in with the mail and gave Papa two letters, one from his sister Rose in America, the other from an old friend in Odessa.

"Aunt Rose sends her love, children," said Papa. "She writes that the snow in New York this year was almost as bad as in Odessa."

"I miss them so much," said Mama suddenly, "and Rose has always been like a little sister to me." Most of Mama's own family passed away before she came to Siberia and she was strongly attached to her new relatives.

"She is afraid Feera and Ida are so big now she won't recognize them if we decide to go to New York instead of Israel."

"Sometimes, Avraham, I wonder…we have no family in Israel, no family at all."

"Well, you know Rose. She has the courage of a tiny cossack," said Papa affectionately. "She'll visit us often."

"It's not the same as having her around. Having anyone around. We'll have no one." Mama's voice, usually soft and calm, carried an unusual tone of panic. I dropped my pencil, scared by the mounting tension. Quietly, Papa picked up the second letter.

"Hadassa, listen to what Bialik is writing from Odessa: 'Wissotzky, you must go to Israel at once, for the sake of your children. I recently received a letter from Dr. Mossinzon. I told you about him, remember? He is the headmaster of the Gymnasia Herzlia. Imagine, a school taught entirely in Hebrew! And the teachers! Mossinzon tells me that some of his teachers are great scholars, university professors, philosophers, artists, writers, and other intellectuals who have escaped persecution in various countries, and now teach the children.' Let's see, what else…he goes on about his new book of poems, just published…then he says 'Wissotzky, the stars in Israel are huge, and the nights are warm. I think you and I should study astronomy together when my wife and I finally settle there. It will probably be only one or two years before we are there with you, sharing this miracle.' He writes well, good old Hayyim

Nahman, doesn't he? They now call him, he says, 'The National Poet' and it makes him laugh…we will have many friends there, Hadassa."

"I really should start brushing up my Hebrew," said Mama and smiled a little. "But I suppose I'll have plenty of time on the road." The first crisis was over.

Later in Israel, Bialik and Papa spent many pleasant evenings stretched on the porch, watching the stars, and sharing poetic remarks about the beauty of the Mediterranean nights. But they never got around to really studying astronomy.

The second crisis involved Papa's father. Grandpa Leib, a widower in his early sixties, lived and practiced medicine in the Ukraine. A towering figure with piercing eyes and a long beard, his life story could make a wonderful script for an adventure movie. To me, the most heroic part was his escape from serving in the Tsar's infamous army.

The Russian soldiers cruelly persecuted the Jews for generations, but they appreciated the skill of Jewish doctors. Once drafted, the doctor served for twenty-five years. Conditions were harsh, and most doctors died before returning to their families. Objection to the draft meant immediate execution—but one loophole existed. If you had any physical handicap, the army didn't want you. So when Grandpa Leib received the draft papers, he calmly went to his medical office, locked the door, injected himself with local anesthetic, and amputated his own left thumb. He couldn't ask another physician to operate on him, because if caught, the surgery would be considered a crime punishable by death. The authorities did not catch Grandpa Leib and he was released from service.

One afternoon I overheard Papa. "Hadassa, I can't leave him alone in the Ukraine and just go. What shall I do?"

"What can you do? We asked him again and again to come with us. He feels he is too old to pioneer."

"All this nonsense about being a burden to us," said Papa irritably. "Some burden! He is as strong as a horse, they need more doctors in Israel, and he will find patients immediately. I am so worried; we didn't get a letter now for three weeks—what am I to do?"

"It's hard to leave a way of life when you are over sixty, and start all over again, Avraham. I understand his reluctance," said Mama sadly.

At this moment the mail arrived, including a letter from Grandpa Leib. Papa smiled. "Isn't it funny? Just as I am fuming over him…Ida, Feera, come here—a letter from Grandpa Leib!"

"Dear children," the letter said. "Forgive me for not writing for a while. You will be happy, though, when you hear the news. Just as my heart was broken over our loss, a miracle entered into my life. I met a wonderful woman, and after all these years alone, we decided to get married. As a child, Sheindle lost her entire family during the pogroms, and lived a lonely life, full of hardships and poverty. When I told her about your plans, her eyes lit up, and she said 'Leib, let's go with them. My lifelong dream was to pioneer to Israel, but I never dared to do it alone.' I explained that we would be poor and have to start all over again, and she said 'do you think I care? I am used to being poor. I'll have a family! That's all I ever wanted, to have a big family and live in my own land!' So I have changed my mind. When you are settled in Israel, let us know and we will come. And you know what else, children? Mark wrote me from America. He said that since his brother Avraham and his family are going to Israel, he will join you there soon with Yeva, his new wife!"

When we were settled for about a year in Israel, Uncle Mark and Aunt Yeva came and lived close by. I was thrilled to have them, because Uncle Mark's hair was even redder than mine—the only other redhead in the family until my own grandchildren were born, and two of them inherited it. A few months later Sheindle and Grandpa Leib followed. We all loved the gentle, kindly woman, and her dreams were happily fulfilled. She truly became a part of our family. Grandpa Leib started to practice medicine, did extremely well, and lived comfortably to the age of ninety-three.

After the illness. Ida's hair had to be cut
because of her extremely high fever.

Grandpa Leib (center) with family

Aunt Rose on a ship, on one of her many trips to Israel

The girls with an uncle and his baby

The girls with their uncle and a family friend

CHAPTER FOUR: PREPARATIONS

The year was 1919. Soldiers started coming back from World War I. The wounded and the prisoners of war also traveled to and from Russia. The military filled the trains to capacity, so civilians found it difficult, almost impossible, to find places. Indefatigably and stubbornly Papa continued his efforts and finally got what he wanted. We were going to travel to Israel.

Not, however, in normal trains, Papa told us. Only cattle trains were available for civilian travelers. Empty coaches, no water, no bathrooms. The railroad managers installed two bunks on each side of the compartment, one above and one below. Instead of mattresses, they hauled sacks filled with straw onto these bunks, and that was the entire outfit they provided.

Worse, if you wanted to leave Russia, your valuable possessions stayed behind. The officials warned Papa that the searches on the road were meticulous, and we should not take money, only food and clothes. Disobeying could cost you your life, but on the other hand, traveling penniless was impossible. No one could help us, and total secrecy regarding such matters was essential. You never knew who talked to the police in this time of suffering and strife.

In the last few weeks before the trip, our horses were sold, all the servants were dismissed, and even our beloved Marusia returned to her parents' home in a distant village, heartbroken over the separation. The curtains were always drawn shut, the houseplants given away to friends.

Except for the lemon tree. It stood bravely under its little lamp, ready for the long trip. When Sasha died, Feera and I were too sick to see him, but Mama told us his last wish. Almost to the end he kept saying that when he got well, and we all went to Israel together, he would take the lemon tree and plant it in a beautiful orchard. So of course we now had to do it for him.

Looking back, I admire my parents and how they involved us with all their tough experiences, dreams, joys, and tragedies. We never lived apart, wrapped in the artificial cocoon of childhood. We shared everything, and for that I thank them to this day. In those dark days of mourning we held together.

One day when all of Papa's patients left, I wanted to visit him in his office. I tried to enter and to my surprise found the door locked, something that had never happened before. Immediately I went in search of Mama to find out what was going on. Mama and Feera were sitting at the dining table, surrounded by an impressive array of loose wool skeins and wound balls. Feera held the wool stretched on her extended arms, and Mama was rolling a ball. She wanted to take a good supply of knitting and crochet materials for the long journey.

"Mama," I said timidly. "Why is Papa's door locked?"

Mama looked at me wearily. "He is praying, Ida, and he does not want to be disturbed."

"Praying? I didn't know Papa ever prayed."

For a moment Mama hesitated. Then the old habit of openness and honesty won. "Well, before Sasha died, I used to believe in God, though I wasn't traditionally religious, and Papa didn't believe in Him. After Sasha died, I stopped believing in God, because how could a merciful God take my son away from me? But at that moment, Papa started to believe in God."

"Why?" asked Feera, obviously bewildered, and dropping her arms with disastrous results to the wool skein. "Why did Sasha's death made him believe?"

"I think because he couldn't bear the thought that Sasha is alone, Feera. He had to feel that someone is looking after a little ten-years old boy…" Absent-mindedly, Mama took the dropped wool and started picking at it, trying to salvage the knotted mess.

"So is there a God or isn't there?" I asked, thoroughly confused.

Mama thought for a long time, slowly untangling the wool.

"You have to make up your own mind, darling. On that question, even a child must decide for herself," she finally said.

"I can't believe in Him just at this moment," said Feera. "I'm too angry with Him."

"I don't know," I said, considering. "Won't it hurt God's feelings if you stop believing in Him?"

"Hurt God's feelings?" Mama asked, startled by the idea.

"Yes, you see, maybe He couldn't help Sasha's death and He feels sad about it too…"

"I always thought He could do anything He wanted," said Feera.

"Who knows," said Mama, throwing the wool into her basket with unusual violence and turning to look at the lemon tree. "Maybe God has feelings, maybe He has reasons, if He exists. I would like to believe that since it would be a comfort, but I don't know. What a mess."

I never knew whether she meant that life was a mess or that the wool was beyond repair. Papa came into the dining room and we had our tea, and spoke of other things.

* * *

Mama sewed a wide belt and put paper money into it. She intended to wear this belt under her clothes. Papa kept raw gold in a small bag around his neck, peasant-style. Mama sewed padded buttons to their coats, and put a gold coin in each button. The night before the trip they baked small rolls all night, and into each roll they inserted two gold coins. They put no forbidden objects on Feera and me. The two of us wandered desolately around the dark, half-empty house, holding hands. If Sasha were there with us, it would have been such an exciting adventure; we would have played such wonderful games. Palma would have been alive, too, and I knew Sasha would have found a way to take her to Israel. Mama could have sewn a little warm coat for her, just like the covering she sewed for the lemon tree. I hoped that somehow Sasha and Palma were together, and that he knew that we planned to take the lemon tree with us. How I missed my big brother, his imagination, exuberance, and joy in life.

I don't remember too much pain in separating from our home. Distant Israel beckoned like a warm, welcoming refuge full of sunshine. We never put it into words until much later, but Russia was no longer our homeland; we became outsiders. Siberia, that magical winter country filled with glowing icicles and stars, betrayed us and turned into a barren wasteland that took Sasha away.

And so equipped with food, clothes, and the lemon tree safely held in Mama's hands, we set out on the road.

CHAPTER FIVE: THE TRAIN

"So how many do you have?" asked Feera in a business-like manner, licking her pencil. "Seven!" I said triumphantly. "Two more than yours!"

"Stop bragging. Yesterday I had nine and you had only six," said Feera. "So tell me your guess for tomorrow, anyway."

Every morning, when Mama, tears in her eyes, tried to shake the lice from our dresses and comb them out of our hair, we competed as to who had more. Feera, who already knew how to write, kept the accounts in her little notebook as to how many lice we had each day, and the projected numbers for the next day.

In each station we searched for water, and filled two jars to last until the next stop, enough for drinking and cooking only. We could not bathe or clean the compartment, and the dirt in the trains was unbearable, so lice thrived everywhere—on the walls, the floor, and in the straw mattresses. The danger of typhoid fever that was carried by lice hovered over us all the time, and no cure for this disease even existed in those days.

But only our parents felt the hardships of the road. I enjoyed myself. The whole family in a miniature room on wheels, meals on the bunks, new people each station—all this fired my imagination and my games became increasingly fantastic, aided by the lack of toys and the limited space and movement for so many months.

And in these miserable surroundings I built my own world. For example, I imagined that a little girl called Hulda lived in one of the corners in the ceiling. Where did I get this name, I don't understand to this day; I never heard even a hint of such a person. One of the wonders of my life occurred when I came to Israel and found out that a settlement called Hulda actually existed.

Every morning, when I woke up to the gray, revolting ugliness of the compartment, I looked at the ceiling corner and said good morning to Hulda. She lived in a tiny house with a red roof, surrounded by a green garden; a beautiful, extremely clean girl, and my best friend. I spent hours upon hours in the corner, talking and playing with Hulda. I still believe that it is possible to find beauty anywhere, if only we know how to properly search for it.

*   *   *

We never changed trains. When needed, the locomotive was changed. At one station, when the train stopped, we saw through the carriage door a kiosk where sweets and newspapers were sold.

"Let's go get some chocolate," suggested Feera. "These things look good."

"Yes, and I want to stroll around a bit," I said. "I feel like walking on real ground."

"Yes, go," said Mama. "Here is some money, but don't remain there for too long. Stay near the train if you take a walk. I don't want to lose sight of you."

Experienced travelers by now, we knew we had plenty of time until the whistle would announce the need to board again. We took our time choosing the sweets, bought whatever we could, and turned around. The train vanished.

I heard the blood pounding in my ears, roaring like thunder, and my chest hurt as if my heart threatened to burst. The station around me shifted in gray, then black waves that engulfed me with dizziness. Helplessly, I looked at Feera. She was pointing at something, unable to talk. At a distance, I saw the last carriage of our train moving far away from us. In unison, we grasped each other's hand and leapt from the platform into the train tracks. Hand in hand, screaming, we chased the departing train, surrounded by other trains moving on interweaving tracks. The loud whistling of these trains silenced our screams. I cannot say how we escaped being run over, nor do I know how long we stayed on the tracks. The nightmarish moments seemed to last a lifetime.

Suddenly, at a great distance, we saw Mama's head poking from the door of our compartment. She was desperately signing to us with her hands to climb on the platform. Somehow we understood. Somehow we obeyed. Leaping in front of an oncoming train, we grabbed the platform and climbed on it, then collapsed on the ground and watched our train returning. It simply changed tracks.

Many, many years passed since that day, and I still dream about a train that is moving away from me and inside it is my entire world.

*   *   *

For a while, the journey went on uneventfully. One night, the itching of the lice bites woke me up. I noticed that the train was not moving, but that happened often. Trying to rearrange the blanket so as to better cover the straw, I heard Papa's voice. It held both determination and apprehension.

Papa stood by the wide-open carriage door and talked into the night: "Hadassa, I am going to throw away the gold from around my neck."

I understood. The searches must have begun. I loved those chunks of gold. I still planned to wear the piece that Ivan Petrovich gave me to balls and parties, looking like a real princess. In whispers, I begged for mercy on the gold. "Papa, what will it do all alone in the dark, on the road between Siberia and China?"

"If they find the gold on my neck, Ida, we will all be arrested."

I didn't know, and he couldn't bring himself to tell me, that the guards did not bother to arrest anyone; they simply brought you to an open field and shot you in the back. He was a good, dear father, entirely devoted to his children, and couldn't bear my disappointment, either. For a second he stood, torn apart by indecision, and then hid one lonely piece in the straw of his mattress and threw the rest into the darkness. Five minutes later two guards entered our carriage. I hid my face to avoid seeing their uniforms and guns. They searched the compartment and told Mama and Papa to turn out their pockets, but didn't bother too much with the mattresses and didn't touch Feera and me. I trembled on my bunk, not even scratching the lice bites, pretending to be asleep. Feera apparently did the same. After an eternity the guards left. They had found nothing.

CHAPTER SIX: ESCAPE

Finally we reached the Manchurian border, the most dangerous point for all refugees planning to leave Russia. The border police in Manchuria performed meticulous searches, followed by severe punishments, particularly for Jewish refugees.

When we descended from the compartment we had occupied for such a long time, I felt I was leaving home. With tears in my eyes I parted from the little imaginary house in the corner of the ceiling and promised Hulda that I would try to find her on another ceiling as soon as I could.

Snow and frost covered the ground, a white, dreary world capped with gray sky. We entered an immense waiting hall, unbearably cold, where hundreds of refugees huddled on the floor with their possessions. All had the same wide-open, scared, tired eyes. Many children cried, but the tension was so great that few adults found ways to relax their children. They just waited, trying not to attract the guards' attention. We quietly joined the throng. Papa sat next to us on the floor; Mama, pale and silent, remained standing, holding the lemon tree tightly.

I looked at the ceiling, halfheartedly hoping to find Hulda and her garden, but the ceiling was very high, dark, and covered with cobwebs. I didn't think Hulda could stand it there. I felt as if darkness invaded my heart as well, the fear paralyzing my imagination.

Then another unbearable thing happened. A policeman motioned Papa to follow him to the men's department. Papa looked back at us, his blue eyes full of pain. "It's all right, girls," said Mama quietly. "You will follow me to the women's department, and soon we will meet Papa in the hall again. Don't worry." At that moment, however, I wasn't worrying about myself, but about Papa. I couldn't bear the thought that he was alone; at least the three of us were together. If only Sasha were here to be with him, I thought, it's so unfair, so unfair, poor Papa, all alone… "Don't cry, Ida," said Mama firmly and put her arm around me. "You will attract attention." Somehow I managed. Mama's immeasurable inner strength never failed me.

We were received by a very tall woman, dressed entirely in black. She even wore a black fur hat, like the hats of the cossacks. Over her forehead peeked a few gray hairs and her face was wrinkled, not with friendly laugh lines around the eyes, but with vicious lines, pointing down around her mouth. She smelled of mildew, and reminded me of *Baba Yaga*, the horrible witch that ate little children in the Russian fairy tales.

This looming apparition went straight to Feera and mumbled: "undo your braids and then take off your clothes." Feera stood naked and shivering from the cold, with only her loose hair reaching her ankles and covering her back. The witch raised her eyebrows with surprise at the magnificent hair, but did not utter even one soft word or try a little smile to relax the terrified child. After Feera was searched I repeated the procedure. When Mama's turn came my heart stopped beating. I observed the speed with which she took off her coat, with the buttons loaded with gold coins, and her stockings' garters which also had some coins in them. The witch took the belt filled with all our paper money immediately. She didn't even bother to check what was in it. She knew. Wordlessly she waited for us to dress and led us to another room.

At least Papa waited there already. It was the office of an official who took care of "criminals" like us, those who dared to smuggle some necessities of life. The official methodically recorded the list of our offenses. Suddenly, he raised his head and looked sharply at us as we stood there, pale and desperate. His eyes rested on the lemon tree in Mama's hand and he asked: "And what's that?"

Mama's fingers went white as she clutched the pot to her heart. We all had the same thought: he will never believe us. He will dig the pot, searching for valuables, and the lemon tree will die of shock.

"That's all I have left from my oldest son, who sowed this lemon tree with his own hands. He died recently," said Mama.

The official's eyes softened. He continued to stare at the little, upright lemon tree. On a chair, next to his desk, the witch left all her loot, including Mama's belt. The official, with a sudden gleam in his eyes, looked at the belt, and then at us again. He seemed to hesitate. Suddenly, he extended his hand to the belt, shoved it at Mama and said: "Take care of the lemon tree and of your daughters." He hastily handed our papers back to Papa, poked his head out of the door and called: "Next traveler!" motioning us to hurry and leave so that no one would witness his act of kindness. He, too, was afraid.

We had no time to thank him. Mama stuffed the belt under her coat to escape the eagle eye of the witch, and we rushed out of the room back to the large, freezing waiting hall. We huddled on the floor very close to each other, covered the lemon tree with its warm scarf, and tried to rest. None of us could sleep in that state of agitation. I didn't want to say anything, being careful to avoid attracting attention, but I had full faith that Sasha's magical lemon tree saved us from severe punishment.

Outside, a snowstorm raged, and throughout the night I heard gunshots, over and over. One woman we knew from the train whispered to Mama, "Hadassa, I heard that they are shooting every person who is leaving the waiting room, and anyone they caught smuggling."

Mama squeezed the frightened woman's hand and didn't answer. It could so easily have been the four of us. For a while, I pretended to sleep, but somehow the tears kept welling in my eyes and a strange pain constricted my chest.

"Mama," I whispered in the dark. "Are you asleep?"

"No, darling. I can't."

"I have to ask you something. It has been on my mind for a very long time."

"What is it?"

"I am afraid to ask."

"Don't be. I will answer if I can. You know I am always honest with you."

"Mama, ever since Sasha died, I had this thought, and today, when Papa had to go alone to the men's department, and Sasha wasn't with him to help him bear it, and he was so alone…"

"Yes, I know. We at least were together, the three of us. I thought about it too, Ida."

"Well, Mama…you had two girls, and only one boy. Did you and Papa ever, well, did you ever wish it was I who died instead?"

Mama jumped to a sitting position and hugged me fiercely. "My poor little darling," she said again and again, her face buried in my hair. "No, no, never. When you love your children as much as Papa and I do, there is no such thing…The love we have for you is separate, complete, unconditional. The loss of Sasha is complete too. Don't ever think this horrible thought again."

I put my head on her shoulder and cried very quietly, so as not to attract attention. Suddenly I noticed a movement and saw that Feera was sobbing into the crumpled bag that served as her pillow. Obviously she had the same thought, and never told me. Mama hugged us both wordlessly. We cried together, the three of us, for a long while. Mercifully, Papa slept. If he had known we felt this way, his heart would have been broken.

The night wore on. There were no rest rooms in the hall; people were afraid to get out and had to relieve themselves where they slept, and the stench was unbearable. I placed my nose next to the lemon tree and finally fell asleep. I believe that sometime during that night I had been completely and finally severed from my childhood. I was just over seven years old.

CHAPTER SEVEN: CITY OF LANTERNS

The pale, bloodless sun illuminated the snow on the ground. Gray, dusty shafts of light entered through the small, high windows, delineating the travelers as they filed in a long line to exit the hall. Carrying our belongings, we listlessly joined the line. The danger was probably over; the shooting stopped during the night. Nevertheless, I doggedly kept my eyes on the ground; the chance of seeing dead bodies strewn around and blood staining the snow terrified me. We boarded the train to begin the long trip to Shanghai.

* * *

Oh, Shanghai in those days! I had no idea what to expect. For some reason, I imagined it as one large pagoda with people who all had the same face and the same clothes. What a mistake!

We entered Shanghai at dusk as thousands of colorful lanterns were lit in succession. Dots, waves and streams of magical lights twinkled and fluttered in every direction. It seemed to me that the city lit the lanterns especially to welcome our family, a fairy city built purposely to cheer sad, frightened children. In reality, Shanghai was a cosmopolitan, large, and beautiful city. It boasted magnificent hotels built in the European style, gorgeously lighted streets, and visitors from all corners of the earth.

Almost delirious with exhaustion, I entered the hotel. It looked like the pictures I had seen of European hotels, with a lobby furnished with sofas and armchairs, a large staircase, and an efficient-looking registration desk. In my half-dream I thought it funny that the entire staff was Chinese.

"Don't sit on the furniture," Mama commanded. Papa was taking care of the registration and Feera and I headed toward an infinitely inviting large sofa, upholstered with red velvet and piled with pillows, cushions, and bolsters of every description.

"Why not?" said Feera. "I am so tired…"

"I know, but you are covered with lice. Don't embarrass us by infesting the hotel. Soon we will bathe."

Bathe? Nonsense. We had not seen a bathtub for months. I looked at Mama skeptically, somewhat annoyed, and suddenly felt extremely proud of her. Dirty, pale, and tired, her dark hair messily tacked with a few pins, she stood erect and dignified, careful of the good name of our family.

We entered our rooms, accompanied by a pleasant, polite chambermaid. We could not communicate verbally, she only spoke Chinese and did not understand any of the languages Mama and Papa tried. It didn't matter. She knew the hardships we experienced on the road from the tales of hundreds of other refugees.

I will never forget the first bath in this hotel. The chambermaid brought kerosene and poured it on my head. She combed it in, then took a handful of a strange-smelling ointment and rubbed it into my scalp and hair. This process, meant for the elimination of lice, was so interesting that I completely forgot my fatigue. After another vigorous combing, she rinsed my hair and washed it two or three times with strong shampoo. Only then I was permitted to sink into the most heavenly warm bath I had ever known. While I was soaking, one of the hotel's employees was sent to buy us new clothes, since every scrap of clothing we had on during the trip had to be burned. The maid braided my wet hair, I put on clean new pajamas, and crawled into a bed covered with soft, white sheets. Not needing to scratch lice bites this night, I slept so deeply I didn't even dream.

I cannot remember the chambermaid's name, but she remained in my heart to this day. Somehow Mama found out her story. She came from a small, distant village, the daughter of wretchedly poor peasants. She even had big feet, the sign of an extremely poor family, because in those days even women of modest means had their feet bound during infancy. She was proud to support herself, but desperately ashamed of her big feet. One dress for work and one for leisure comprised her entire wardrobe, but she always managed a scrupulously clean and neat appearance. At the early days of our stay in Shanghai, I could not tell the Chinese people apart. Slowly I began to notice their faces, to differentiate, and how I loved the friendly maid's beautiful face!

Without a common language, this kind woman tried to please us in so many ways. One evening, when her grueling workday was over and she had already taken her bath, she took Feera and me to her room to show us how she washed her own hair. Her modest, clean room was filled with objects I did not know or recognize, totally different from our European-style rooms. The simple arrangement was attractive and restful. The maid filled a large porcelain bowl with fragrant oil and put it on a small table on which stood a single flower in a white vase. She undid her luxurious black hair and passed a wooden comb through it. Bending over the bowl, she dunked her hair in the oil and swished it vigorously, then wrung the oil out. She quickly mounted the hair on her head in the shape of a pretzel, stuck two long pins in it—and the ritual was completed.

From our window we saw the bustling street, much like a large stage with varied and strange spectacles. The rickshaw struck me as the most amazing surprise. A wheelbarrow on two wheels and a roof, a padded seat, and instead of a horse—a man! The first coolie I saw, thin and sweaty, ran with his shirt open to the wind, breathing hard. I saw circuses in Russia, with animals trained to behave like humans, to dance on two legs, or to drive a bicycle—but I had never seen a man trained to be a beast of burden. Tears choked me.

But I was a child, and despite the pity I felt enormous curiosity. I looked at the rickshaws every morning from my window until I got used to the idea. I was encouraged by the fact that some of the coolies smiled cheerfully as they were paid; perhaps they did not think about their job as humiliating and I was just imagining things again? The next step involved persuading Mama to take us for a short ride in a rickshaw. She clearly didn't want to, but finally succumbed to my begging. We climbed on one and started out, but after a "trip" of about a hundred meters, she stopped the coolie, paid him, and we got off. For a few minutes she was silent. Then, holding back the tears of pity, she said fiercely, "I am not ready to eat their 'roaches', and I don't want to ride their people!"

Secretly, I was glad we got off the rickshaw. I felt nauseous throughout the course of this "trip." I tried—and didn't want any more of that.

I enjoyed strolling in the streets much more. Food was sold from small stalls in all street corners, including eels, oysters, and shrimps. These were the "roaches" Mama referred to; she could not abide seafood except simple fish, and as this food also seemed so foreign to a girl from Siberia, I never ate anything exotic in Shanghai and stuck to Western foodstuffs. But the new and exciting toys that were sold there! I had never seen such marbles before, every size and all the colors of the rainbow, transparent, opaque, swirled. I started collecting them, not so much to play, but to admire their beauty and arrange them in different configurations. Feera fell permanently in love with the tiny, elegant boxes, made from cinnabar, enamel, wood, and silver; she continued to collect pretty boxes even as a mature woman. And the marvelous dolls, all with Chinese faces and so elaborately dressed in silks! We wanted everything.

By now, however, money started to run out. Papa, with his usual enterprising spirit, decided to earn some. Right there in the hotel, he took out his dental tools and arranged a makeshift dental office. He told everyone that he started seeing patients, and in a few days had a large practice comprised of the hotel staff, guests, and even many Chinese townspeople who felt like trying exotic dentistry from Russia.

We stayed in Shanghai for a month, a month of rosy days and peaceful nights. While waiting for the ship that would take us to Egypt, we met many children from various countries, made friends, and enjoyed new adventures every day. For a while, I was so busy I even stopped looking for Hulda. We forgot the lice; our health improved. Mama,

Feera and I wandered about all day enjoying ourselves, and at night Papa joined us to explore English theater and Chinese dance companies. It was so good to see Mama looking beautiful and well-dressed again, her dark hair elegantly done and her warm gray eyes just a tiny bit less worried.

All the while, the lemon tree did very well on the window sill, enjoying more sun than it could get on the train from Siberia. It even unfurled a few new, delicate leaves. Interestingly, the hotel staff treated it reverently, with innate understanding of its being both a living, beloved plant, and a cherished symbol of hope.

Official papers from the Chinese consulate in Irkutsk

The Hongkew market in Shanghai

CHAPTER EIGHT: THE SHIP

Finally, the festive month in Shanghai came to a close; the ship that was to take us to Egypt had arrived.

The first ship in my life! A floating palace. Halls furnished in European style, crystal chandeliers, gilded walls. What excitement.

We did not travel first class, of course; despite Papa's patients in Shanghai, our huge expenses exceeded our income. So we had to separate again. Papa shared a cabin with three other men, and Mama and us shared one with a lovely Japanese lady.

As usual, the separation worried me, bringing back the anxiety and rage over Sasha's death. I left our cabin, letting Mama and Feera attend to our things while I followed Papa to check that he did not feel too lonely in his cabin as he settled in. He seemed to be all right, so I just sat and chatted with him as he unpacked. Suddenly Feera burst into the cabin in high excitement.

"Ida, come at once, you must see the strange things the Japanese lady is doing—"

We ran back to our cabin. All seemed peaceful and normal. The lemon tree already stood on the little table under the porthole, and the Japanese lady and Mama conversed amicably in French while arranging their belongings. I looked at Feera skeptically, seeing nothing extraordinary. The lady hung a number of elegant kimonos on wooden hangers. Then she sat on her bunk and like a magician performing an elaborate sleight-of-hand, started taking object after object out of her wide sleeves! I stared as small candy boxes, a fan, cosmetics, money, a mirror, and a tiny book with an illustrated cover made their appearance. The lady laughed at our amazement, turned the sleeve inside out and showed us a capacious hidden pocket in the silk lining. She opened the little book with the illustrated cover, and I saw that nothing was written on the creamy white pages. Motioning us to approach her, she tore out the first two pages and rubbed them on our noses—each page, made of the softest rice paper, was saturated with fragrant face powder! We were speechless with admiration for this great invention. Noticing that, she fished deeper into the sleeve, produced two little identical books, and gave one to each of us. I ran to the mirror to admire my elegantly powdered nose, but Feera grabbed me.

"Wait! Look at her bed," she said. "That's what I called you for."

Something strange happened to the bed; the pillow disappeared, and was replaced by an intricately carved wooden box.

"She sleeps on this, she already explained it to Mama when you were out. Let's ask her to show us."

"No," I said, intimidated. "We'll wait. Maybe she was just joking and she'll laugh at us."

Later at night we stayed awake to spy. The lady came in, and arranged herself for bed with a long and interesting beauty ritual of makeup removal, cleansing, washing, putting on various lotions, and powdering, entirely unaware of our heartfelt appreciation. We never saw such a thing at home; Mama didn't use makeup. Like most ladies at that time, she believed that only sparkling cleanliness and simple elegance and neatness of dress were morally acceptable, with perhaps just a touch of powder on the nose. When she finished her preparations, the lady reclined on her back, placing her big, elaborate hairdo right into the little wooden box. This way the hairdo remained neatly arranged and she didn't have to redo it every morning. As I looked at her, sleeping peacefully, I had a funny, improbable thought. What if she had lice? What would she do if her head itched?

The experiences I had during the extended journey on the trains served as a life-long lesson: I learned to enjoy little things, to be happy over every small comfort, and most important, to greatly appreciate people who treated me kindly. On the ship, the travelers became a big family, and so the long trip turned into a stay in paradise.

One morning, I noticed a most bizarre contraption on deck—a small room without a ceiling, its walls and floor made of cloth. I went to investigate, and saw some people hosing water into the incomprehensible thing. This ship had no swimming pool, but the resourceful Japanese travelers created a freestanding pool from thick, watertight canvas. Splashing in the pool turned out to be great fun, but I discovered that redheaded people with delicate skin must watch for the sun as well as the frost. My poor nose, now safe from freezing, turned bright red from sunburn, while Feera's golden skin tanned beautifully. "How unfair," I wailed, and Mama laughed and smeared suntan oil on me. "But your new freckles look so good with your green eyes," said Papa convincingly. "I am sure they are fashionable in the Middle East, where the sun is so strong. You will be greatly admired." We dunked in the pool and played with the Japanese children whose language we did not understand except "arigato" (thank you). They were incredibly polite and friendly children, and loved to give little presents. One particularly curious present I still remember. They gave us small balls, each about the size of a thumbnail and made of some rubbery material, half green and half white. You put it under your tongue and played with it, swishing it in and out, much like using chewing gum. For the entire time I didn't search for my Hulda. I was happy.

Occasionally we stopped in a port and were permitted to have a short visit ashore. I don't remember much, as impression upon impression already crowded my short, eventful life. I retain one hazy memory from Hong Kong. A few ladies, wearing gorgeous silk dresses, stopped us in the middle of the street to express their admiration of Feera's incredible chestnut hair. They had never seen, they said, such long hair on a Western child. I also recall a scene from Singapore, a land of unimaginable tropical beauty, and the sweet and tangy taste of my first pineapple, picked there straight from the plant and sliced, the golden, fragrant juices dripping on my hands.

The lemon tree, bravely withstanding all the hardships of the road, continued growing on the ship. Mama caressed its leaves every morning, and the warm weather must have been good for it; it was spring, the blooming season for citrus trees. All the travelers on board heard its history and shared our feelings. Many came to visit it every day, some from curiosity and some because our faith rubbed off on them.

*   *   *

Finally, we arrived at Port Said, in Egypt. As usual before any new event, I couldn't sleep all night, but the excitement of being almost there, almost in Israel, kept me from feeling even the slightest degree of tiredness. Feera and I went on deck at dawn. We wanted to see the sun rise on the approaching land.

"Do you think we will be in Tel-Aviv this afternoon?" I asked.

"Definitely," said Feera. "It's really close, Papa said. Remember the map? Port Said seems like a step away."

"I want to go straight to our new apartment," I said enthusiastically. "Papa said he'll give us all the keys, and we can find out which key fits into each door and closet. That will be such fun."

"The sun is so bright here," said Feera. "Just like Sasha used to tell us."

Suddenly, without warning, we both stood there, holding hands and sobbing. Sasha's memory and the pain of his loss were somewhat dulled during the trip. But here we were, where he longed to be, and it all seemed so unfair, so unfair… "We'll plant the lemon tree in the best orchard, just like he wanted," said Feera, wiping her eyes. "Stop crying immediately. Mama and Papa will be sad if they see us."

"Maybe we'll do it tomorrow, if the orchards are close by," I said.

CHAPTER NINE: ANOTHER VARIETY OF SHIP

Unfortunately, it didn't happen quite that fast. The ship didn't even go into the port. It was moored far away, and we had to go to the shore by boats. Secretly, I was terrified of the small boat, bobbing on the blue waves, and it took all my will power not to disgrace myself in public by refusing to go into it. Mama supported me through the short trip, holding me close, as I experienced seasickness that never hit me on the large ship. Mercifully, we quickly arrived to the shore of Port Said, a large, bustling city.

Here we had to wait as well. We lived in a hotel where many Jews stayed on their way to Israel, waiting for the official papers to be set in order. Again, Papa stacked a few crates in a street corner, covered them with clean white sheets, and added a wooden chair to the arrangement. Before he could finish organizing the dental tools on the crates, a line of Egyptian patients formed in front of the makeshift office. They were smiling and friendly despite their obvious toothache and poverty, and paid whatever they could afford.

Papa was tremendously excited by the Red Sea and the Suez Canal, and we did some sightseeing in Port Said. I can't recall how Mama and Feera felt, but I was tired from all the new impressions, and retained no strong memories from Egypt. I only remember the impatience; I wanted to arrive, I wanted so much to reach Israel. Our trip lasted an entire year.

*   *   *

One day, Mama, Feera and I drank our tea on the hotel's porch. We almost had it to ourselves, the only other occupant a very young man, almost a boy. I had often seen him before, but never spoke to him because he wore traditional Arab clothing and I assumed we had no common language. We could see Papa, who had just finished treating his last patient, cleaning and packing his tools. Suddenly a man in a white suit approached him. They spoke for a few minutes and the man handed Papa a sheet of paper. Papa entered the hotel, sat down, and with a look of total despair slapped the paper on the table. Mama picked it up and read carefully, slowly.

"It can't happen," she finally said, gently laying it on the table as if it threatened to explode. "Not when we are that close."

We looked at Papa, too frightened to ask.

"It's a government paper, and they won't let us go to Israel," said Papa, and translated it for us.

The letter declared that our papers were not in order, and therefore, the government could not take it upon itself to sign a permit for crossing the border to Israel. They gave us two options. We could return to our port of origin, Shanghai, on the first ship that would become available, and would have to present the officials with a proof of our intended trip. Or we could go to court, right there in Port Said, and try to reverse the decision by submitting additional papers. Either way, the choice had to be made within a couple of weeks.

"We can't have additional papers, because such papers don't exist," said Papa. "Our papers are in perfect order."

"I wonder what they really want," said Mama.

"Money, I think," said Papa, "It's probably the work of some petty officials trying to extort money from refugees. And we don't have any funds."

"But we can't go back to Shanghai," said Mama. "We don't have papers to reenter there."

"Of course not. They won't let us in. Ever since the end of the war, ships full of refugees are turned away from one port after another because they don't have the proper papers."

"We may have to write to your family in America."

"What's the point? We can't arrange anything in such a short time."

I waited for the line that always followed difficulties. One of them would say, "There has to be a way," and the other would suggest a course of action, and something would inevitably be attempted. But both my parents were silent. There seemed to be no solution. Cold despair made my stomach sink. After all our efforts, we were finally defeated.

"Excuse me, Dr. Wissotzky, may I join you?" said a quiet voice behind us in perfect Russian. "I have overheard your conversation." It was the young man that I had thought was an Arab.

"You know my name?" asked Papa, perplexed. "Who are you?"

"You were right about the situation, Dr. Wissotzky. The officials pick on some refugees within every new group. For some reason they selected you, perhaps they think you have a lot of money or rich relatives who can be approached. Your papers are most likely just fine; you will have no trouble in Israel when you cross the border. To answer your question, I work for a Zionist organization that helps people like you in difficult situations, and we make sure we know everyone's name and history. It's best if you don't know my real name or the name of the organization at this point."

"But you are a boy! How old are you—sixteen, seventeen?"

"Looking young helps, no one suspects me, and I am, actually, almost eighteen. There are others like me."

"What shall we call you? And how can you help us?"

"My code name is Shemariahu. My plan may involve serious danger, but it's the only way. I have to get you to Kantara, where you will intercept and board the train to Tel-Aviv. We have our people there, and your papers will present no problem. Of course you can't use the normal train from Port Said, because of the permit that the local officials are denying you."

"But won't they look for us if we don't present them with the proof of going back to Shanghai?" asked Papa.

"We regularly forge such proofs. We will send it to the officials in a week or so, and you will already be safe in Tel-Aviv."

"So how do we go to Kantara?" asked Mama apprehensively.

"By camels, Madame Wissotzky."

"Camels?" She stared at him, startled.

"You will join a camel caravan. A large caravan, including some Druse and Moroccan travelers. Many of them are light-skinned and have blue eyes, so you will not be noticed, as long as you wear Arab clothes. We will have to dye the little one's hair black, just in case, even though she will wear a headdress. Her hair is just too noticeable."

Black hair! Caravans! Ali Baba! I was overjoyed.

"What danger, precisely, are we talking about?" asked Mama, sighing with resignation. I think she felt that she had experienced enough adventures for a while.

"The caravan goes through the desert, of course, and often there are clashes with robbers. Occasionally, soldiers check the caravans, which is much worse."

"Ah, well," said Mama, rising to the occasion. "We had our experiences with border police and survived it. As for riding camels, I loved riding horses around the estate that my father managed. It can't be too different."

"It is entirely different," said Shemariahu cheerfully. "Camels move and sway. That's one of the reasons they call them 'ships of the desert,' but you'll do fine, I am sure."

"Can I keep the black hair when it's all over?" I asked, sticking to the really important matters at hand. "No one in Israel really knows that I have red hair—"

"Ida!" said Mama, scandalized by my impropriety. "A lady only colors her hair when it's absolutely necessary!"

* * *

The ship of the desert and I looked at each other with mutual distrust. Undeniably beautiful, sporting long eyelashes and blue and gold jewelry, she had this haughty expression and seemed to sneer at me. Also, she was rather tall. How was I to climb such a beast? There were no ladders in sight. The camel, on the other hand, probably realized that despite my jet-black hair I was not really an Arab, and she obviously didn't appreciate foreigners who didn't know how to ride properly. The owner spoke to her softly, and to my amazement, she kneeled gracefully on the ground. The owner helped Feera and me onto the comfortable rug that covered the sand-colored fur, and once we were firmly established, the camel rose back to her feet.

Mama rode her camel impressively well, and Papa and Feera didn't do too badly. At first, I had a terrible attack of seasickness from the camel's motions. She really swayed crazily, much like a ship. In addition, she had a peculiar smell, not really unpleasant but strong, and it did not help my queasy stomach. Eventually I learned to move with the rhythm rather than resist, and the nausea passed away.

I don't remember how long the trip lasted; time passed as in a dream. Sand and sky blended and the enormous distances matched the snowfields of Siberia for sheer vastness. Here and there some palm trees dotted the unchanging landscape, surrounding a water hole. Glaring, brutally hot sun. A couple of times we saw riders at a distance, but mercifully, they never approached our caravan. I only remember one moment, when, suddenly, unexpectedly, terror hit me.

"Feera," I whispered. "Do you think they will search us in Kantara?"

"Shemariahu told me the guards only spoke to the men, never to women and children, and usually just to the caravan's chief, so they probably won't even bother Papa." She didn't sound very convincing.

"I keep thinking about Manchuria," I confessed. "I am terribly scared."

"The border police and that Baba Yaga woman? Yes, I thought about them too. I keep thinking, maybe Shemariahu didn't tell us the truth. Maybe he didn't really work for a Zionist organization at all. Maybe he just lured us into the hands of some robbers..."

"What can they do? Do you think they shoot people here, too?"

"I don't know, Ida. I am horribly scared, too, and I feel so tired in a strange way. Sometimes I don't believe we'll ever get to Tel-Aviv."

It was evening when we reached Kantara, a miserable little train station in the middle of the desert. Two guards, their guns casually slung over their shoulders and their smiles missing many teeth, exchanged a few friendly words with the chief, and showed him where to put up the tents for the night. No searches, no questions, they indiscriminately stamped whatever piece of paper was handed to them without so much as glancing at it, got some cigarettes from the chief, slapped him on his back, and went back to their post. I loved them.

On the ship Sikaka-Mara, going to Port Said

With a group of refugees in Port Said

A camel caravan in Port Said

CHAPTER TEN: HOME

A tiny train, as if made for elves, brought us from Kantara directly to Tel-Aviv.

The thing I remember most was the light. The glorious light of the Israeli sun, turning everything into gold. The train station contained one hut surrounded by a small garden, its only ornament a quantity of spotlessly clean shells lining the garden paths. I had never seen such shells before; white as sea foam, to me they were pearls.

We could travel the short distance to the hotel in the primitive mode of transportation available at the station—a big wagon hitched to two horses. But Papa didn't want it. He insisted that he must take his first steps in Israel with his feet treading its earth.

And so we arrived by foot, a small caravan headed toward a tiny town. I looked at Tel-Aviv and her little white houses—and fell in love; until today, there is no city in the entire world that I love as much as my Tel-Aviv.

I had no idea, at the time, how much culture already flourished in the little settlement. Someone had started a library on one side of town. Classical music was played in makeshift halls, plans made for introducing opera. Passing the new little music academy, you could hear the children learning to play the piano, flute and violin from musicians who once played in symphony orchestras in European capitals. You could learn ballet and modern dance from a lady who had once danced with the famous Ballet Russe, and be instructed in a number of languages by immigrants who came from many lands. In one of the little houses someone wrote magnificent poems in the ancient language that was undergoing such a transformation it became new and fresh. In another, a great artist painted the blue sea and white dunes. Every evening, people gathered to discuss politics, literature, philosophy, and art in many of the modest living rooms.

Within a few days we had a sweet, clean little apartment with whitewashed walls and floors of polished yellow tiles. As promised, Papa produced the keys, gave them to Feera and me, and we ran happily around, fitting them into doors and closets. Papa took out his dental tools and immediately was ready for business. Mama unpacked our possessions and quickly stuck a few onions in the built-in planters on the porch; this was important—the green, fresh tops were essential for serious cooking. Of course, I secretly resented the scrubbing she gave my hair to remove all traces of the glorious black henna rinse, but being a redhead again did not matter a great deal at that happy moment. It was so good to feel permanently rooted in one place.

When everything was neat and ready, Mama looked around her as if something was missing. "What's the matter," asked Papa, worriedly. "One thing is an absolute necessity of life and we must get it immediately," said Mama. "We are going out directly to buy a samovar!"

We cheered in unison and went out to the little store to purchase our new samovar. We spent some time choosing just the right one, a dignified brass affair that looked much like the old friend we left in Siberia. When we were ready to take it home twilight already filled the sky with pink and blue tints. People sat on every porch, drinking tea. Others strolled in the street. If they wanted to visit, they just stopped, came up, and had tea with their friends. No one felt the need to let anyone know in advance; it seemed the friendliest arrangement imaginable, and people, some of them total strangers, called at us again and again to join them and have some tea and cake. When we finally got home, we sat the samovar on the dining table, and there it stood majestically, humming cheerfully and musically to itself. Our home came alive.

Feera and I shared a little room overlooking the lovely back yard, where palm trees, vines, and flowers grew in messy profusion. We had white spreads on our beds, small chests of drawers by their side to serve as both nightstands and storage units, and two little wooden desks and chairs. I felt so important, having my own desk, where I would some day do my homework.

We longed to go to school, learn the language, make friends, lead a normal life. Our parents told us so much about this wonderful, famous school they wanted us to attend—the Gymnasia Herzlia, named after Theodore Herzl, the visionary Zionist. A beautiful, white, spacious building with two towers, it loomed over the tiny houses and contained all twelve grades. It was, however, very late in the year and Mama wasn't sure how strict the rules were about such matters, particularly for students with our peculiar history.

Mama held our hands and took us to the Gymnasia to register. We entered the large yard, where students of various grades were playing together during recess. In the middle of the yard we saw a tall man bent over a little boy, with a ring of screaming children surrounding them. We approached cautiously. The man straightened up, holding a coin which he apparently extracted from the boy who nearly choked himself swallowing it. The boy coughed and spluttered hysterically.

"Calm down, nothing happened, you're fine, you silly monkey," said the man affectionately, in Russian, and patted the boy's head. "The work I have to do around here…Now, if you solemnly promise me to never swallow a coin again, I won't tell your mother."

"I promise, Dr. Mossinzon," said the boy.

"So run away and play."

"Dr. Mossinzon," said Mama behind his back.

The headmaster of the Gymnasia Herzlia turned. He was a dignified, tall, handsome man, and had a long black beard, cut square.

"I am Hadassa Wissotzky," said Mama. "These are my daughters Feera and Ida, nine and eight respectively. They have missed an entire school year on the road from Siberia, and they don't speak any Hebrew. They are anxious to go to school, and I would like to register them, though I am aware it's almost summer vacation. Would this be in order?"

Dr. Mossinzon bowed gallantly. "Madame Wissotzky, in a school where the headmaster must regularly fish diverse objects out of children's throats," he said seriously, "anything and everything is in order. The girls are welcome to start tomorrow morning."

Later, we happily found out that the teachers were flexible and accustomed to new students appearing any time during the year. And a large number of the students were refugees just like us.

The next day we went to school, hand in hand and rather nervous. Feera belonged in a higher grade and the separation alarmed us, our circumstances having made us unusually dependent on each other. However, the night before we made a solemn pact to succeed in the new environment, and I intended to keep to it. Bravely, I entered my classroom. The sun streamed through the tall windows, illuminating the spacious room with long shafts of light. Maps and pictures of various Zionist leaders hung on the white walls, together with colorful pictures drawn by the students. A few potted plants grew on the windowsill, and a vase of red and yellow wildflowers stood on the teacher's desk.

As the teacher introduced me to the class, in Hebrew and in Russian, I stood by the blackboard and looked at the children, sitting two by two at wooden desks. A sea of new faces, confusing, even frightening. I felt so alone; I desperately wanted Feera. The teacher pointed me to a seat next to a pretty girl who had no partner. As soon as I sat down someone said something in Hebrew and the whole class laughed and started chanting. I was ready to be horribly offended, when the girl smiled and said in perfect Russian, "Don't worry. They are laughing because my name is Ada, and they are chanting 'Ida and Ada, Ida and Ada. They think it's funny how our names match." I laughed, relieved, and looked at her closely for the first time. Ada seemed oddly familiar. The soft ash-brown curls, blue eyes, and regular features; the little pink dress, so clean and neat, with a sparkling white collar…
"Hulda!" I said, catching my breath. "You look just like Hulda!"

"Hulda? Who is Hulda? Surely you don't mean the settlement we have here, named Hulda?" Asked Ada.

"What? There is a settlement in Israel by the name of Hulda?"

This was too much to digest at once. I gaped at her, almost overcome by all these mysteries. "I'll tell you all about it at recess," I said weakly.

"You have such beautiful red hair," said Ada with sincere admiration. "I always wanted red hair. It's so fashionable in Europe, you know."

That settled it; I knew we were friends for life. And we still are best friends, two grandmothers, so many years later. Ada's curls are snow-white now, and she is just as beautiful today as she had been then.

At recess, before I could explain about Hulda, Feera ran over to introduce me to a new friend. "This is Leah," she said. "And she doesn't speak a word of Russian. Would you believe, she was born here! Her family came to Israel hundreds of years ago from Sepharad, which is Spain, so they call themselves 'Sephardim,' isn't that something…"

"Feera, how did you find out? You say she doesn't speak Russian!"

Feera stopped to think. "I don't know. We somehow talked, maybe my other new friend, Ora, translated. Do you know what her name means? 'Ora' is 'Light' in Hebrew. She was born here, too, but she speaks a bit of Russian with her parents."

"My name is Yafa," said another girl with black curls and a red ribbon. "It means 'beautiful' in Hebrew."

Ada laughed. "That's how I learned Hebrew, too. You just talk to people, and suddenly it happens." Ada Fichman, the daughter of a noted poet and world traveler, already spoke fluent Russian, Yiddish, German, and Hebrew, and a smattering of French and English as well. And she knew what she was talking about. In no time Feera and I felt quite comfortable and started picking up the language with the speed only children are capable of. We were so busy, so happy. We were home.

A typical apartment house in Tel-Aviv

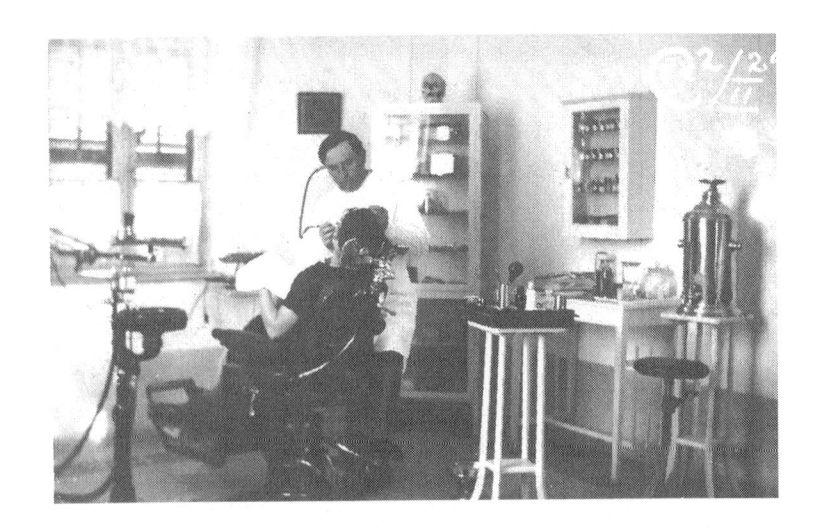

Avraham's dental office in Tel-Aviv

In the park at Yehuda-ha-Levi Street.

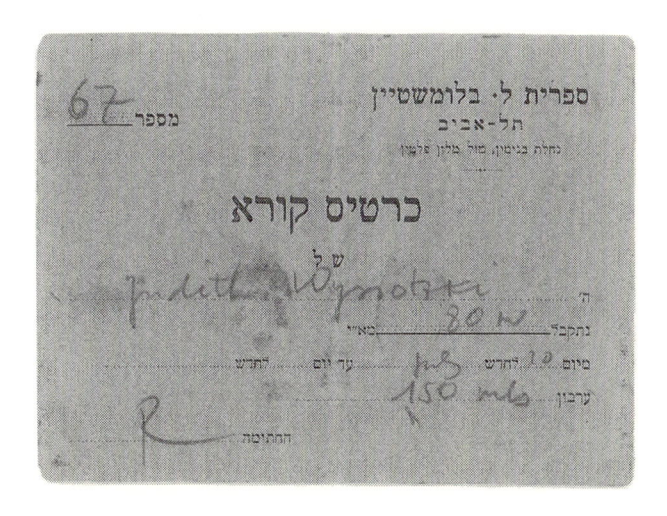

An early lending library card

Ida with a friend, dressing up

Sailing on the Yarkon River with friends

Ida and Ada as teenagers

CHAPTER ELEVEN: SASHA'S DREAM

The lemon tree reached Israel in all its green glory, a pioneer of the famous "third wave of immigration" in everything. It arrived exactly as Sasha dreamed, to the sun, the warmth and the light. The tree had a place of honor in the new home, the best ornament in the two rooms we inhabited; it made us feel that Sasha came with us. We thought we'd keep it a little longer before transplanting it, to make sure it continued healthy and well.

After a short time, during the hot Israeli summer, the lemon tree's leaves began to yellow. Mama looked at it, pale and worried. She did all that could be done but the tree went on yellowing. So Mama brought the pot to a professional gardener; he listened to the story of the long trip from Siberia, checked the leaves and pronounced: "The change of climate killed the plant. There is nothing I can do."

Mama walked home quietly, thoughtfully, holding the pot close to her heart. Feera and I, who accompanied her to that nursery, walked silently by her side. A second funeral procession for Sasha.

At home, Mama put the tree on the windowsill and collapsed on a chair. Papa came out of his office. Feera told him what the gardener said.

"No," he said with determination. "I don't care what he said."

"Avraham," said Mama wearily. "He must be right. It is a known fact that a change of climate can kill a plant."

"I don't care if every horticultural book or learned professor of botany said that, Hadassa. This is not a plant; this is Sasha's dream. The lemon tree must be planted in an orchard."

So we took the lemon tree to the citrus orchard of a good friend who knew how we felt about it. We planted it and prayed.

Weeks passed, one of us visiting every day, making sure the tree had all the water it needed. There seemed to be no change in the tree's condition. The leaves stayed yellow, and didn't get either better or worse. Summer came to an end and nothing happened.

In the meantime, despite our worry, we had a wonderful time this first summer. Our new friends introduced us to the fascinating, unique culture and every day brought some adventure or revelation. One day, our Sephardic friend Leah invited us to supper to experience their interesting cooking. She took us into the garden and picked a bunch of glowing orange flowers from the climbing squash. I assumed this would be the table decoration, but instead of looking for a vase she handed them to her mother in the kitchen. The mother washed the flowers with clean water, dipped them in batter, and started frying them right in front of our disbelieving eyes! The supper was absolutely delicious, but I don't remember the other dishes. Eating these dainty flowers made me feel like a fairy from the Arabian Nights.

We registered at the tiny library and found to our joy that it had many Russian books, among other languages. We would be well supplied until our Hebrew improved. Of course we also borrowed Hebrew books, it was such fun.

We bathed in the warm Mediterranean and loved it; the sea was often green and calm, without a single wave, and gave off the scent of watermelon. By now I knew I had to carefully watch for sunburn with my white skin, and always wore big hats and some covering. Still, I no longer minded my looks so much since Ada, the great traveler and my best friend, had told me that red hair was so fashionable in Europe! Perhaps it was a good thing, I thought, that Mama did not let me keep my black hair after the trip from Egypt. It would have been awkward to suddenly change. And maybe I would really be very pretty some day and go to balls and parties? Ada and Feera said they were sure of it. At night, our friends took us to enchanted moonlit walks on the white dunes, with the air scented by the flowering wild jasmines; I found these walks utterly romantic and magical. Time passed quickly.

"Feera," I said one day. "Let's go to the orchard and tell the lemon tree we are starting school again tomorrow."

"It's autumn already," said Feera. "Isn't it strange? Still so hot! Remember how cold it got this time of year in Siberia? You know, Ida, we may never see snow again."

"Who cares? I like the white sand dunes much better. Besides, if you really want snow, it falls in Jerusalem every six or seven years, they tell me. Next time it happens, we can go."

We went to the orchard and knelt by the lemon tree for the daily inspection. Something seemed different.

"Can this be true?" I whispered and looked at Feera. She saw it too. Her golden skin turned white, drained of blood. We both stared at a tiny, almost invisible green dot that appeared on the top of the little tree. "Come, let's go and get Mama and Papa," she whispered back. "They must see this—this miracle—right away!"

*   *   *

Today, the beautiful, stately lemon tree still grows in the center of the orchard and gives the best of lemons every year. Young trees are regularly grown from its cuttings, flourish in numerous other orchards, and in turn provide more cuttings that grow into new trees. Through this endless succession, Sasha's lemon tree will live forever, as long as the sun shines on the state of Israel.

EPILOGUE

By Ilil Arbel

If you enjoyed the story of the Wissotzky family and developed some affection for them, you may perhaps wish to know a little about the family's later years. They are no longer with us, but I am sure Ida would not object to this addition to our narrative. She always loved a happy ending.

* * *

As the girls matured, Israel of the thirties, forties, and fifties experienced financial austerity. There were no excesses of any kind, not even real luxury. And yet, despite war and trouble, it permitted a fascinating and unique way of life, where East and West freely mingled.

Riches meant little, while education and culture meant everything. Teachers of all levels were highly respected. Perhaps this was the result of so many pioneers belonging to the "Russian Intelligentsia" and later the arrival of the extremely well-educated German Jews. Naturally, you wanted to be comfortable, but being really rich would be slightly embarrassing. It cannot be denied that many people experienced real poverty at times, particularly on arrival to Israel. Well educated and carefully brought up young girls went to work as cleaning women. Older women came to the more affluent houses to do the laundry, a very hard job since washing machines did not exist. You sloshed your hands in the almost boiling water in a round pan made of zinc, and scrubbed every piece. Men took any type of menial job they could get, mostly in the construction of homes and roads. Both genders worked in factories, on the land, and in all the services. Poverty was hard, as it always is, but menial labor was not a source of humiliation in this slightly Utopian environment.

A famous anecdote recalls a philosophy professor who came to Israel with his wife, a teacher. She opened a thriving high school, but what kind of a job would be available to a professor of philosophy before the first university was created? Well, after much thought, Max decided to become a street sweeper. In those days, you did it with a straw broom, at night. What could be nicer for a philosopher? The job would gives him solitude, time to think, and would free at least part of his days for writing!

Hardly any fancy foods were available, but you could always have the best fruit and vegetables, fresh milk and other dairy foods, and beautifully baked bread. As human nature dictates, despite the availability of fresh produce, everyone adored the canned foods that were sometimes sent from America, if you were lucky enough to have relatives there. These canned goods were considered rather exotic. Children in particular loved the canned fruit, and marshmallows were thought a rare delight. Since many of your new friends came from every corner of the globe, the sheer number of cuisines that you could sample at their tables was amazing—and the variety defeated the austerity. Dining grew to be cosmopolitan. Little restaurants sprang everywhere, sharp Eastern spices mingling with the heavier scents of the East European cooking.

The toy shops were often almost empty of merchandise—but the children spent most of their afternoons playing together in the yards and parks, running around in the fresh air, or going in groups to the beach. You could climb fences or trees, and gorge on the wild mulberries, guavas, and figs that grew everywhere. In other words, you learned to socialize instead of choosing to sit in front of a TV—which was not even allowed to exist in Israel until much, much later.

Books, original and translated, were everywhere—bookstores, research libraries, lending libraries, school libraries, and street stalls. You had to be careful with them since they were very expensive. In most libraries, repairing the books was a big part of the librarians' job, and on the first day at school, every child was instructed to wrap the school-issued textbooks right away.

For the adults, social life blossomed—balls, parties, constant small gatherings. People dropped in on each other at any time to chat and drink coffee, and since many houses did not possess a telephone, without checking in advance. If your friends were not at home, you visited someone else, or strolled to the beach and sat in a café overlooking the water, where you were sure to meet some acquaintances, or make new friends. Many charming little bands from all over the world came to sing in these cafés, and people were exposed to popular music from places they had never heard about. You could hear the children of East European Jews singing the rousing songs of a Mariachi band, or little Yemenite children singing Hebrew songs that were set to the ponderous, though melodious, Russian music.

The theatre thrived, and some truly great actors graced the stage, performing both original and translated plays. The concert halls were always full, and musicians from every country came to perform to one of the most enthusiastic audiences in the world. Divas came to sing in the modest little opera house, defying the unsophisticated conditions.

Art flourished. It was strongly influenced by Professor Boris Schatz and his unique Arts and Crafts school *Bezalel*, founded in 1906. The school was named after the Biblical artist and craftsman Bezalel Ben Uri, the man who built the first Tabernacle. With this historically-oriented spirit, Schatz believed that arts and crafts were two sides of the same coin, and every student in his school had to study both. His romantic and innovative vision combined Hebrew, Zionist, and Jewish symbols, and the school included numerous departments. This innovative approach gained him the nickname "The Israeli William Morris." Naturally, over the decades much of his vision underwent transformation, and many other artists continued to express their own unique vision.

Literature burst into new life. Great writers and poets produced works in Hebrew, a language that grew richer every day with the development of the nation. The new culture constantly added material to the millenniums of the Jewish commonwealth of learning and love of books.

People worked hard to make a living, but not in an overstressed, workaholic style. Life was balanced. For example, many people went to the beach for a brisk swim before starting work, thus beginning the day with a pleasurable, invigorating activity. Others went there after work was done, in the pleasant coolness of the sunset. At dusk, even after the hottest days, a fresh breeze blew in from the Mediterranean. Lunch was the main meal of the day, and then everyone had a siesta, a most intelligent habit in such hot weather. For two or three hours the stores were closed, offices emptied out, and the bustling streets turned suddenly silent under the scorching sun. Work resumed later in the cooler hours of the afternoon, the workers feeling refreshed rather than fatigued. After work, many people met friends at the outdoor cafés, and enjoyed the parade of people passing by before going home to a very simple supper.

Often, people gathered to listen to special programs on the radio together, many of the women bringing their needlework with them. Needlework was an extremely popular pastime. Special little stores sold you tablecloths to embroider, knitting and crochet supplies, and all sorts of exciting notions. There were no glossy craft magazines, but the owners could actually give you the knitting instructions, hand scribbled quite accurately on a piece of paper; a lost art in our world.

The one trouble that always loomed, always threatened, was war. The tragedy of losing loved ones could never be far away from anyone's thoughts. The only saving grace was the wholeness of purpose that people felt in their lives. They traveled unthinkable distances because they finally had a country and a government for the first time in two thousand years, and they loved both. Certainly, the actions of the government were often criticized and questioned, but it was still their own. Isolated, surrounded by a huge number of enemies, people drew together. The fallen were heroes, not victims. The sacrifices were honored; the grief was shared.

Despite the constant war threat, economic hardship, and political trouble, people enjoyed their lives, their work, their families, and their friends. They had a dream that was not yet spoiled by harsh realities. And nothing in this world gives so much joy in life as an intact dream.

*   *   *

Dr. Avraham Wissotzky did not live a very long life. Having suffered from tuberculosis as a child, his weak lungs claimed him in his late fifties, but not before he contributed both professionally and personally to many lives. In addition to his successful career as a dentist in Tel-Aviv, he was a wonderful writer and published both fiction and non-fiction books. As I briefly mentioned in the introduction, I am currently translating into English two of his novels, *Tel-Aviv* and *Green Flame*, both telling the fascinating stories of pioneering families. Some day I plan to publish *The Lemon Tree* and these two novels together as a very special edition, which will be named *The Aliya Trilogy*.

Dr. Wissotzky continued to be a wonderful father and grandfather, and his grandchildren benefited greatly from his wondrous storytelling, complete with his curious ability to draw pictures of Aesop's Fables with his arms around the children as they sat on his lap. His dental office was a place of magic for them, full of interesting and absorbing old objects, including a fascinating real human skull that never failed to scare them a little. You can see this skull in the photograph, standing in its place of honor on the cabinet.

Hadassa Wissotzky lived to her mid-seventies. She battled with cancer in her fifties, and—quite an amazing feat in those days—won this battle. She healed and lived on, until eventually she was claimed by pneumonia. Hadassa continued to be a tower of strength, a councilor, and a friend to all who knew her. A practical, highly intelligent, and utterly charming woman, she was the center and the core of her family and of a large group of loyal and loving friends. Hadassa never lost her green thumb, her love of good cooking, and her talent for intricate crafts; she had done her best to generously teach her skills to anyone who was interested. As a grandmother she simply had no equal.

Feera grew up to be as lovely and intelligent as a young woman as she was during her childhood. She studied business in London, and there she met her future husband. Moshé Mishory was studying to be a veterinarian, but Hadassa objected to the profession, on the strange and funny grounds that it would make him smell like horse manure! In a more serious vein, and practical as ever, she suggested to Moshé, "why not switch to dentistry, and then work with Avraham?" It seemed like a good plan and Moshé switched fields. He never regretted it and indeed became a successful and well-respected dentist. Dr. Mishory was a most cultured and well-educated man, with a deep interest in history and archaeology. Feera and Moshé had two boys. As was customary in those happy, family-oriented days, the Wissotzky and Mishory families shared a huge multigenerational home, a place full of joy, fun, and learning.

And now to our heroine, Ida. Old Ivan Petrovich's prophecy came true—she grew up to become a celebrated beauty. People traveled from other towns just to see the flaming-haired, green-eyed, ivory-skinned young woman, who was also intelligent, musical, and artistic. She was widely painted and sculptured by well-respected Israeli artists. Ida's dream of balls and parties came true—the Wissotzky sisters were immensely popular during this very social era in Israel.

In the Gymnasia Herzlia Ida received an exceptionally good education, since many of the teachers there were scholars of high standing who had escaped persecution in other countries. In addition to the regular course of studies, she developed great interest in art and design, and studied music and languages. She inherited her father's talent for storytelling, but specialized in the oral rather than the written medium. During her school days she developed friendships that lasted a lifetime. Amazingly, some of them were with the same little girls she met during her first year in school. You can see the photographs of some of these girls as they grew up to become stylish young women.

When she graduated from the Gymnasia Herzlia, Ida worked for a while as her father's dental assistant and decided she liked the profession. She traveled to the University of Nancy in France, which had a good dental program, and very soon was the center of a large and cheerful group of friends. It should be noted that one of the first things she did in Nancy, just after getting an apartment, was to rent a piano which had to be hauled up to the fifth floor. Living without a piano seemed inconceivable.

One of the most appealing anecdotes regarding her unusual beauty and charm occurred in Nancy. It happened at the most unexpected setting of a large Zionist gathering where a very great man, Ze'ev (Vladimir) Jabotinsky, came to give a lecture and participate in a banquette.

In America, Jabotinsky was probably best known for his script (based on his own novel *Samson*) for the famous movie *Samson and Delilah*. However, he was a towering figure in Zionism and was quite revered. He was also a prolific writer. One of his more romantic and fanciful books, *The Five*, was autobiographical. The heroine, a rather magnificent red-haired young woman named Marusia, was a most alluring character, if somewhat overly romanticized. It was not a secret that Jabotinsky was thoroughly in love with her in his younger days and her identity was hotly speculated upon by his readers without success. The tale was made even more heart wrenching since Marusia dies in the book during a horrible fire, occurring when the wide and flowing sleeves of her elegant negligee catch fire as she cooks breakfast for her children. Sacrificing herself to save her children, she dies and leaves broken hearts all around her. Many readers sobbed over this book.

As Ida entered the banquette room with a group of Zionist friends, Jabotinsky was already seated at the table. He raised his head to see the newcomers, and suddenly stood on his feet, seemingly struck by the proverbial lightning. Everyone watched as he gazed at Ida for a long moment and whispered "Marusia…" He took some time to recover sufficiently to start the lecture, and Ida's friends never let her forget this interesting little triumph.

Later on at Nancy University, when she was twenty-two, Ida met her future husband, Dr. Leibek (Arieh) Rosenfeld. A dentist and an oral surgeon, he was only twenty-eight years old, and already was promoted to the high position of the head of a clinic at the dental department.

Leibek, a very handsome, dark-haired young man with warm brown eyes, was a cosmopolitan, sophisticated individual, highly intelligent and blessed with a wonderful sense of humor. He was born and raised in Poland, where he received an exceptional education and was fluent in various languages. His uncle sent him to study dentistry, and Leibek planned to return to Poland and join his uncle's dental office. However, after he and Ida were engaged, he soon went to Israel to meet her parents, and fell in love with the beautiful country, the warm water of the Mediterranean, the little white houses among the dunes, and the tiny though sophisticated city of Tel-Aviv. He refused to leave.

It was extremely fortunate that they decided to marry and stay in Israel, because all of Leibek's large family, including his dentist uncle, died in the Holocaust. Leibek was the only one to survive of the entire family.

He was an amazing linguist. Already fluent in Polish, French, Yiddish, German, Latin, and Greek, Leibek quickly picked up Russian, so as to communicate better with Ida's parents who still liked to speak Russian to each other. Naturally, he also learned Hebrew. Years later, visiting his American daughter-in-law, he picked up English in one month, from only conversations and television.

They were soon married. After a wonderful tour of Europe, including such exciting adventures as climbing Mount Vesuvius and the Swiss Alps, drifting through the Blue Grotto in Capri, and enjoying the marvelous cuisine of Belgium, not to mention its famous chocolates, Ida and Leibek settled very near the rest of the family on the bustling Allenby street in Tel-Aviv, and Leibek opened his office. He became a very successful dentist and oral surgeon, eventually heading the Municipal Department of Dentistry in Tel-Aviv. Ida's home was a showcase, where she invested her superb sense of design to create a most unusual, even striking décor, which at the same time was full of comfort and ease.

Ida and Leibek had a son and a daughter. They were exceptional parents, raising their children in an atmosphere of love, freedom, and respect. I hope you will be pleased to hear that they led a very happy life, full of wonderful friends, varied interests, travel, and culture.

Dr. Avraham Wissotzky

A portrait of Feera

Feera as a young woman

Ida on the ship heading for France

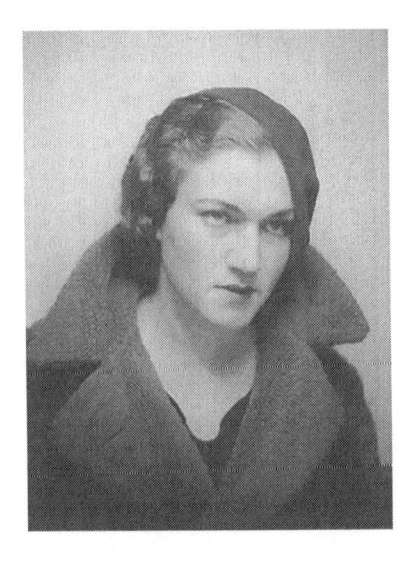

Ida in Nancy

Leibek in Nancy

Ida's bust, created by an Israeli artist

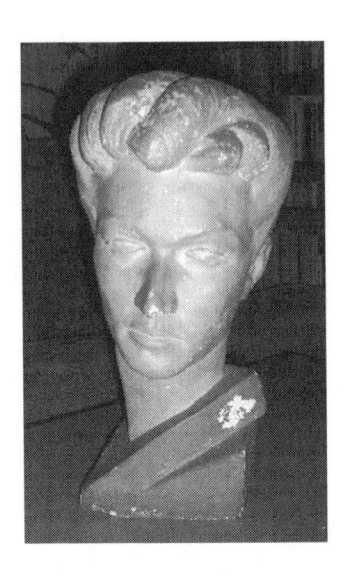

Another bust modeled after Ida

Ida, painted by an Israeli artist

Allenby Street, 1933

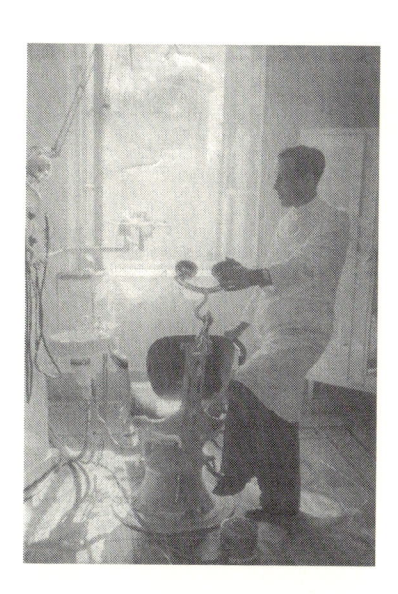

Leibek's office in Tel-Aviv

Feera and Moshe Mishory

At a seaside café in Tel-Aviv

Ida and Leibek with their children

Yafa, Ida's childhood friend, a stylish young woman of the 1930s

Ora, Ida's childhood friend, with Ida's son (right) and her own son

86   The Lemon Tree

The Habima Theater in Tel-Aviv

Ida's and Feera's older children

Ida's and Feera's younger children

The sisters

0-595-33982-4

Made in the USA
Lexington, KY
16 January 2013